Birthdays

AROUND THE
WORLD

JENNIFER KLEIMAN

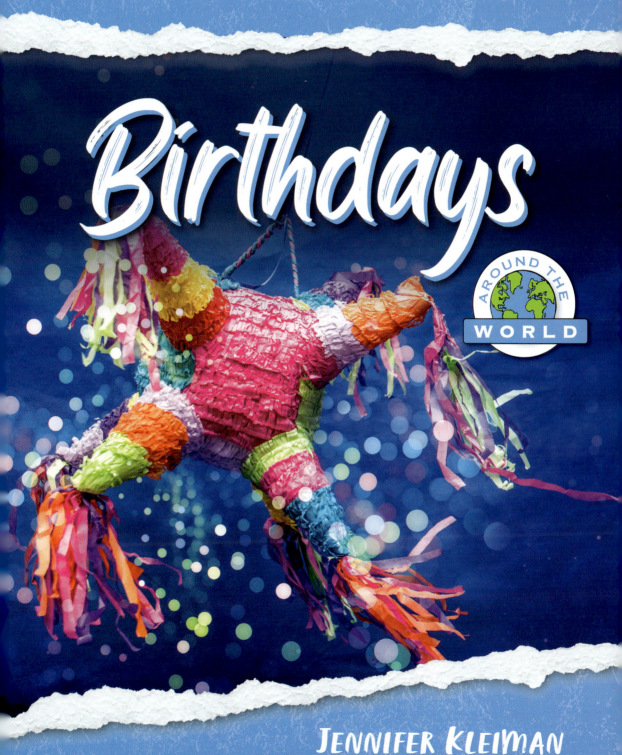

45TH PARALLEL PRESS

Published in the United States of America by Cherry Lake Publishing Group
Ann Arbor, Michigan
www.cherrylakepublishing.com

Reading Adviser: Beth Walker Gambro, MS, Ed., Reading Consultant, Yorkville, IL

Photo Credits: © clicksdemexico/Shutterstock, cover, title page; © Jfunk/Shutterstock, 4; © pikselstock/Shutterstock, 6; © Laktikov Artem/Shutterstock, 9; © pikselstock/Shutterstock, 10; © Ljupco Smokovski/Shutterstock, 11; © Krakenimages.com/Shutterstock, 12; © wbgorex/iStock.com, 13; © Shutterstock, 15; © Pixel-Shot/Shutterstock, 16; © Jennifer Kleiman, courtesy of author, 17; © Dayna Light/Shutterstock, 28; © Tamonwan_Newnew/Shutterstock, 21; © KIBOK RHEE/Shutterstock, 22; © whyframestudio/iStock.com, 23; © James Dalrymple/Shutterstock, 24; © William Borney/iStock.com, 26; © Steven Harewood/Shutterstock, 27; © Dietmar Temps/Dreamstime.com, 28; © Gabriel Q/Shutterstock, 29

45th Parallel Press is an imprint of Cherry Lake Publishing Group.

Library of Congress Cataloging-in-Publication Data

Names: Kleiman, Jennifer, 1978- author.
Title: Birthdays around the world / written by Jennifer Kleiman.
Description: Ann Arbor, MI : 45th Parallel Press, 2025. | Series: How the world celebrates | Audience: Grades 4-6 | Summary: "Another year older, another year wiser-birthdays let us celebrate who we are and who we are growing to be. Readers will explore how people around the world celebrate their birthday, and the customs and traditions that define those celebrations. This hi-lo narrative nonfiction series celebrates diverse cultures while highlighting how expressions of joy and connection are all part of the human experience"-- Provided by publisher.
Identifiers: LCCN 2024036510 | ISBN 9781668956564 (hardcover) | ISBN 9781668957417 (paperback) | ISBN 9781668958285 (ebook) | ISBN 9781668959152 (pdf)
Subjects: LCSH: Birthdays--Juvenile literature.
Classification: LCC GT2430 .K54 2025 | DDC 394.2--dc23/eng/20240918
LC record available at https://lccn.loc.gov/2024036510

NOTE FROM PUBLISHER: Websites change regularly, and their future contents are outside of our control. Supervise children when conducting any recommended online searches for extended learning opportunities.

Table of Contents

DID YOU KNOW? The rarest birthday is February 29. That's because February usually has 28 days. Every 4 years, it has an extra day. It's called Leap Year. Only 1 out of every 1,460 people are Leap Year babies.

Introduction

A birthday is the **anniversary** of the day you were born. An anniversary marks the date of a special event. Think of it as your own personal new year. You reflect on how you've grown. You look forward to another year. Family and friends celebrate with you.

Many cultures all over the world celebrate birthdays. They share some birthday **traditions** in common. A tradition is a practice passed down over time. Celebrating with loved ones is a common birthday tradition. So is giving gifts. Yet, not everyone shares the same traditions. Many cultures have their own ways to celebrate. They have special ceremonies. They celebrate on different days. Some cultures don't celebrate at all.

Chapter 1

An American Birthday

Tyra rises early. She is too excited to sleep. Today is her 13th birthday. She is officially a teenager.

Tyra's father greets her in the kitchen. "Happy birthday!" he says. "I've made your favorite breakfast."

A stack of chocolate chip pancakes is waiting for Tyra. A "Happy Birthday" balloon floats above her chair.

Her father waves an envelope in the air. "Grandma's card is here!"

Every year, Tyra's grandmother sends a birthday card. Tyra opens the card. There is a gift card inside from Tyra's favorite store.

Tyra gathers everything she needs for the pool. In the past, Tyra had birthday parties at home. This year, she is having a pool party. Her father has rented the community pool. The area is decorated with balloons and streamers. A "Happy Birthday" banner hangs from a wall.

Tyra has invited her friends from school. Guests place gifts and cards on a table as they arrive. Music is playing. Kids are splashing. The crowd gathers around the birthday girl when she arrives. They wish her a happy birthday. Then Tyra joins them in the pool.

"Food's here!" Dad carries a stack of pizza boxes. Tyra sets out the paper plates and napkins. She pours drinks for her guests. Everyone lines up. One by one, the guests file back to their tables. They sit down to eat. Everyone is wrapped in towels.

The day is getting late. It is time to open gifts. Tyra opens them one at a time. She holds each one up for the guests to see. She thanks the person who gave her the gift.

DID YOU KNOW?

Americans love to send birthday cards. Americans buy about 6.5 billion greeting cards each year. Birthday cards make up 20 percent of those sales. Including money or gift cards is a popular tradition.

Tyra's aunt brings out the cake. Thirteen sparkling candles pop and sizzle like fireworks. Tyra smiles awkwardly while people sing "Happy Birthday."

"Make a wish!" says her aunt. "But don't tell anyone, or it won't come true."

Tyra closes her eyes and makes a wish. She blows out all 13 candles in one breath. Everyone claps.

Tyra's aunt hands her the knife. It is **customary** for Tyra to cut the cake. Customary means the way it is usually done.

Tyra cuts a neat chocolate wedge. She slides it onto the plate. "Okay," she says. "Who wants cake?"

CHAPTER 2
A Mexican Birthday

The sun has barely risen. Music drifts through Marcelo's window. This can only mean one thing. Today is Marcelo's birthday!

Marcelo's family **serenades** him. A serenade is music played outside. It is often played under someone's window.

The twins' voices are the loudest. They are singing "Las Mañanitas." Waking up to it is a birthday tradition. Marcelo's brother plays his **guitarrón**. Tomás strums the large, deep-bodied guitar. His parents and the twins sing along.

After breakfast, Mamá sends Marcelo on an errand. The house is quiet when he returns. He walks outside to the garden.

LAS MAÑANITAS

"Las Mañanitas" is the birthday song in Mexico. It is often sung to awaken the person. Sometimes it is sung in an early morning serenade.

SPANISH

Estas son las mañanitas
que cantaba el Rey David.
Hoy por ser día de tu santo,
te las cantamos a ti.
Despierta, mi bien, despierta.
Mira que ya amaneció.
Ya los pajarillos cantan,
la luna ya se metió.

Que linda está la mañana
en que vengo a saludarte.
Venimos todos con gusto
y placer a felicitarte.
Ya viena amaneciendo,
ya luz del día nos dio.
Lavántate de mañana,
mira que ya amaneció.

ENGLISH

This is the morning song
that King David sang.
Because today is your saint's day,
we're singing it to you.
Wake up, my dear, wake up.
Look, it's already dawn.
The birds are already singing,
the moon as already set.

How pretty is this morning
that I come to greet you.
We all come with joy
and pleasure to congratulate you.
It's already dawning,
giving us the light of the day.
Get up in the morning,
look, it's already dawn.

"Surprise!" Two dozen faces pop up.

A surprise party! Everyone is there. His aunts, uncles, cousins, and his dear *abuelita*. Marcelo hugs his sweet grandmother.

The twins run up to Marcelo. "We surprised you!"

Marcelo's family joins the twins. They make a tight circle around him. Everyone is smiling. They are holding *cascarones*. They crack open the eggshells over Marcelo's head. He is quickly covered in **confetti**. Confetti is made of bits of paper. It is a fun and festive way to celebrate the occasion.

Cascarones are also used to celebrate Easter in Mexico.

Marcelo's uncle calls the children to him. "*!Vamanos, niños!*" he says with a wave. "Let's go, kids!"

A rainbow-colored piñata hangs from the tree. It is shaped like a donkey. Marcelo's uncle blindfolds him. He spins Marcelo around 3 times. Then he sets him loose. Marcelo grips the stick tightly. He swings and misses. Marcelo takes a deep breath. He swings once more. The stick strikes the piñata hard. The sound of candy patters to the ground like rain. All the children fall to their knees. They stuff their pockets with treats.

Marcelo's mother brings out 2 cakes. Marcelo enjoys his second round of "Las Mañanitas" that day. After the singing, it is time for one final tradition.

"*Torta en la cara!*" they all chant. "Cake in the face!"

Marcelo's abuelita flashes a devilish smile. This is her favorite part. She shrugs, as if to apologize. Then she gently pushes his face into a cake. Everyone laughs and cheers. Marcelo laughs too. He licks white frosting from his cheek. "It's delicious!"

Marcelo's younger brother got cake in the face from Abuelita last year.

DID YOU KNOW? A doljanchi is a first birthday celebration. It is a **milestone** birthday in Korea. A milestone marks a new phase of life. A doljanchi marks the beginning of childhood.

Chapter 3
A South Korean Doljanchi

Ji-hye wraps her **chima** around her waist. It is a traditional Korean skirt. Today, the whole family will wear traditional clothing, or **hanbok**. It is her brother's doljanchi. Minho turned 1 on Wednesday. Today is Saturday the 15th. It is an **auspicious**, or lucky, date in Korea. That's why Ji-hye's parents chose it.

The Kims have spent many days preparing. They hung colorful banners and lanterns. They decorated the table with flowers. They arranged decorative dishes of rice cakes, fruit, and sweets. They stacked the "Dol" table high with food. This symbolizes a life of **prosperity** for the baby. Prosperity means wealth and success.

DID YOU KNOW?

The won is the Korean dollar. In Korea, people often give money in multiples of 10,000 won. That's equal to about 7 U.S. dollars. 10,000 is considered a lucky number.

Ji-hye is there to greet the guests as they arrive. She is holding little Minho. He is also dressed in hanbok. The guests have brought gifts. Some give items the baby needs. Others give gold and jewelry. They also bring gifts of money. Some of the elders offer blessings.

Ji-hye's parents have hired a professional photographer. She takes pictures as the guests arrive. Everyone wants a picture with Minho in his hanbok.

The **doljabi** is the most important part of the day. It means "first birthday grabbing." Several items are arranged in front of Minho. The item he grabs will predict his future. There is a pencil. It means Minho will be intelligent. There is a coin for wealth. A stethoscope means he will be a doctor. A microphone predicts he will be an entertainer. Finally, there is a piece of thread. This means Minjo will live a long life.

The guests make a circle around Minho. Everyone is encouraging him to pick a different item. Ji-hye chose the microphone for her doljanchi. She loves to sing. She hopes Minho chooses the microphone too. They can start a band when he is older.

Minho reaches out a plump arm. Ji-hye holds her breath. Minho's hand lands on the microphone!

It is time for the feast. There are rice cakes, noodles, and savory pancakes. A steaming pot of seaweed soup is placed before Ji-hye. Seaweed soup is served every birthday. It symbolizes what mothers go through to bring children into the world.

After the meal, there is karaoke. People take turns singing popular songs to music. This is Ji-hye's favorite part.

"Go on, Ji-hye," says her mother. "Show everyone how well you can sing."

Ji-hye takes the microphone. She chooses a song everyone knows. Her voice is bright and clear. Great-grandmother hugs her tightly when she finishes.

"You have a beautiful voice, Ji-hye. I knew you would."

"How did you know, Great-grandmother?"

"Your doljanchi predicted it, of course!"

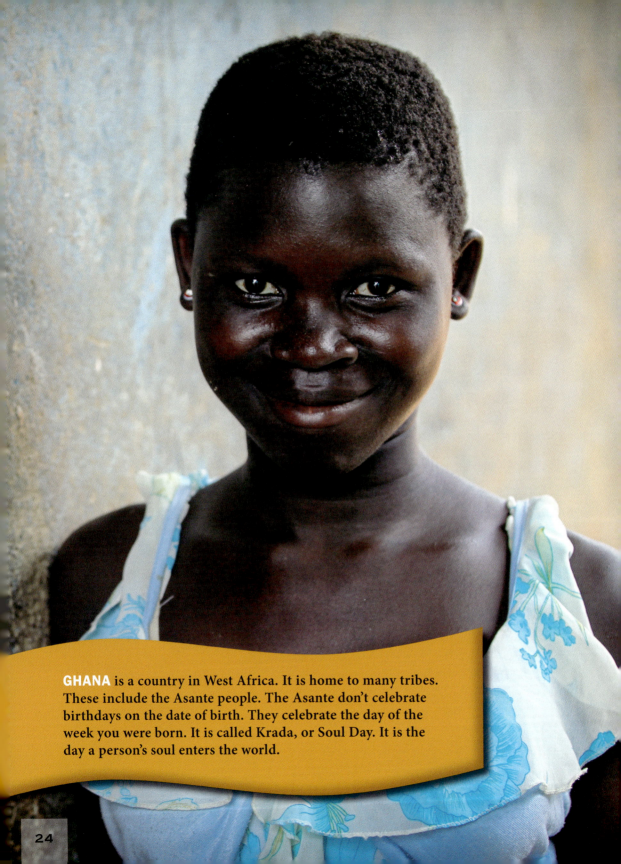

GHANA is a country in West Africa. It is home to many tribes. These include the Asante people. The Asante don't celebrate birthdays on the date of birth. They celebrate the day of the week you were born. It is called Krada, or Soul Day. It is the day a person's soul enters the world.

CHAPTER 4
A Soul Day Celebration in Ghana

Abena rises with the sun. A new sun means a new day. Today is Tuesday. It is her krada, or Soul Day. Abena was born on a Tuesday.

Abena begins her day with the cleansing ritual. It is a tradition among the Asante people. Abena washes herself with a special leaf. The leaf has been soaked in water overnight. The ritual is symbolic. It is meant to **purify** her soul. To purify means to make clean.

"Abena, it is time to wake up." Maame is waiting in the kitchen.

"*Mema wo awoda pa,*" she says. "Happy birthday."

"*Medaase, Maame,*" Abena replies. "Thank you, Mama."

Maame has prepared a traditional birthday treat. *Oto* is made from mashed sweet potato and palm oil. Maame serves it with boiled eggs. In Ghana, it is a traditional birthday treat for children. It is served to them in the morning.

Abena washes her hands before she eats. Mama puts the bowl of oto in the center of the table. Everyone digs in with their right hand. Using the left hand is a sign of disrespect. Abena presses the sweet potato mixture into a ball. Then she takes a bite. It tastes sweet and delicious.

Later that day, Abena prepares for the feast. Her family is hosting it in her honor. Abena carefully drapes the white kente cloth over her body. It is tradition for her to wear white today. White is a **spiritual** color. Something that is spiritual relates to the soul. This kente cloth belonged to Abena's mother. She is careful to treat it with respect.

Many in the village have come to the feast. They are all dressed in their kente. Maame has made more food than anyone can eat. In Ghana, this is tradition for any celebratory occasion. There is fried fish, goat meat, and mountains of jollof rice. There is *fufu* and goat light soup. Maame makes the best fufu in the village. It is made with a root vegetable called cassava.

After the meal, it is time for dancing. Guests dance the *adowa*.
This is a popular dance among the Asante people. It is famous for
its hand movements. Every gesture has a meaning.

Abena breaks away with the other girls. They are going to
play *ampe*. It is a popular birthday game. It involves clapping,
jumping, and kicking.

"It is Abena's day," says Yaa. "She should be the first leader."

Every girl gets a turn to be the leader. The leader with the
most points wins. The girls laugh because they have lost count.

Abena walks home that night with a joyful soul. Another Soul
Day has ended.

ACTIVITY:
HOW TO MAKE A BALLOON PIÑATA

Learn how to make your own piñata using a balloon.

MATERIALS:

- Water
- Flour
- Balloon
- Scissors
- Newspaper
- Paint
- Tissue paper
- String or twine
- Candy

INSTRUCTIONS:

STEP 1: Mix 1 part water with 1 part flour to create a paste.

STEP 2: Blow up the balloon and tie at the end. Use the scissors to cut newspaper into enough strips to cover the balloon several times over.

STEP 3: Dip newspaper strip into paste. Squeeze off excess paste. Apply to balloon. Allow to dry.

STEP 4: Repeat Step 3. Create 3 to 4 layers, allowing each layer to dry before adding another. Leave an opening at the top for candy.

STEP 5: Let dry for at least 24 hours. Then pop the balloon and decorate the piñata with paint and tissue paper.

STEP 6: Make two holes in the piñata for the string. Thread the string through the holes. Tie the string ends together to make a loop.

STEP 7: Fill the piñata with candy. Hang and enjoy!

LEARN MORE

BOOKS:

Asante, Erica. *Threads of Me: Kente for Show and Tell,* Golden Cocoa Books, 2022.

Kaminski, Leah. *Hola, Mexico.* Ann Arbor, MI: Cherry Lake Publishing, 2020.

Orr, Tamra B. *Korean Heritage.* Ann Arbor, MI: Cherry Lake Publishing, 2018.

ONLINE:

With an adult, explore more online with these suggested searches.

- "Games of Ghana—For Kids!" Landmark Center

- "Ghana Facts for Kids," Kiddle

- "How to Make Cascarones," Instructables

GLOSSARY

anniversary (aa-nuh-VER-suh-ree) the yearly return of the date of a special event

auspicious (aw-SPIH-shuhs) suggesting that future success is likely

chima (CHEE-mah) a traditional Korean skirt

confetti (kuhn-FEH-tee) small bits of paper made for throwing

customary (KUH-stuh-mair-ee) commonly practiced

doljabi (DOL-juh-bee) a Korean ritual practiced on a child's first birthday; means "first birthday grabbing"

guitarrón (gee-tah-ROHN) a large Mexican 6-string acoustic bass guitar

hanbok (HAHN-bow) traditional Korean clothing

lineage (LIH-nee-ij) people descending from one common ancestor

milestone (MYE-uhl-stohn) an important point in development

prosperity (prah-SPAIR-uh-tee) condition of being successful or thriving

proverbs (PRAH-verbs) wise sayings

purify (PYUR-uh-fye) to make clean

serenade (sair-uh-NAYD) performing music for someone, especially when outdoors

spiritual (SPEER-ih-chwuhl) relating to the spirit or soul

tradition (truh-DIH-shuhn) a belief or practice passed down over time

INDEX

ABOUT THE AUTHOR

**Jennifer Kleiman** has worked in educational publishing for more than 20 years. Today, she is a busy writer and editor, working on her second novel. She lives in Chicago, in a rickety old house, with her wife, 2 cats, a dog named Helen, and a yard full of chickens.